THE GREEN ACTIVITY BOOK

Meryl Doney

Illustrations by
Linda Francis
and
David Mostyn

It's not easy being green

Hopping you like this book!

CONTENTS

A LION BOOK
Oxford · Batavia · Sydney

Maybe it *is* getting easier to be green. After many years of hard work by such groups as Friends of the Earth and the World Wide Fund for Nature, people are getting the message that the environment matters. Schools are doing projects. Television and radio regularly feature 'green' issues. And governments are concerned about environmental problems.

The more we learn about it, the more we realize that we live in a beautiful, delicately balanced and fragile world. It's a bit like a spider's web. Touch one single thread and the whole structure trembles. I believe the reason why everything hangs together is that it was designed that way—because God made the whole universe. It has the mark of the maker all through it. He didn't just bring it into being with a 'big bang' at the beginning: he is the power that keeps it going, from the smallest atom to the largest galaxy.

I also believe that God has made people to be responsible for ourselves and our planet. If this is true, we have fallen down badly on our responsibilities. Selfishness and greed have done their worst in the world. God has allowed this to happen because he has always given us the freedom to make our own choices. But we must live with the consequences, and the world we now live in is a confusing muddle of good and bad effects. It's hard to untangle them. It's even harder to begin to put things right, but at least we now realize that we must try—before more damage is done.

But you don't have to believe that God created the world to want to make it a better place. We are here, alive and aware, and the future of our planet is very much our concern. Every one of us can do something practical to help. That's where I hope this book will be useful. And I'm sure you'll soon discover that being green can be fun!

Your world needs you! So get started right away, mobilize your friends, your school, your town. Who knows, eventually the whole country may join in. Then we may stand a chance of making the world the beautiful place God intended it to be.

About this book

As well as giving you facts about many different 'green' issues, this book is full of ideas for projects to work on with your friends, things to make and do, games to play and quizzes to involve the whole family.

Inside the back cover you will find patterns for making a poly-styrene superglider and a set of clothes for a teenage doll.

You and your friends can play 'Go for a green earth'. This exciting new board game about the environment is printed on the outside back cover.

Inside the front cover is a ready-made poster for you to use if you have a conservation or ecology group. You can use this again and again if you photocopy all the posters you need before filling in any details. At the end of the book you will find a list of addresses of various organizations with a concern for the environment.

So read on, get busy and have fun being 'green'.

All things by immortal powe
Near and far
Hiddenly
To each other linked are,
That thou canst not
stir a flower
Without troubling a star.

Francis Thompson

How do frogs feel about the way we treat the planet?

Hopping mad

RECYCLING

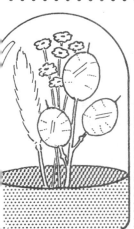

The word re-cycling means 'going round again'. We use it for the process of taking something that has been used and treat-ing it so that it can be used again. For instance, some manu-facturers sterilize and re-use glass bottles and jars. Now we are beginning to realize that we could save re-sources by recycling other things such as paper, card and aluminium cans. We can also do our own recycling in a small way by finding new uses for things we usually throw away. Here are just a few ideas. See if you can think of others.

Plastic Bottles

Clear plastic fizzy drinks bottles with a plain domed base make attractive display cases. Soak the bottle in hot water until the plastic base comes off.

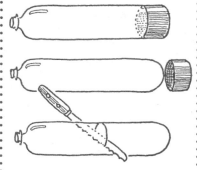

Ask a grown-up to cut across the bottle half way down with a bread knife. Using the end of the bottle as a guide, cut out a circle from a clean polystyrene meat tray.

Wedge this circle into the base. Stick your display, such as a favourite ornament or a posy of dried flowers, on to this circle. Finally, push the plastic dome over the top.

Large plastic detergent bottles with moulded handles make very useful pooper-scoopers for dog owners. Holding the handle, cut

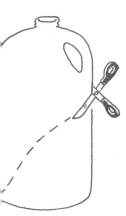

out a shape like an old-fashioned scoop. Cut a spatula shape out of the base of the bottle. Pierce a hole in the end of the spatula and tie it to the handle with a long piece of string. Both can then be hung up outside when not in use. Remember: always wash your hands after using this.

Tins

For a handy desk organizer, arrange and glue together some tin cans (they need to be washed and empty). Use clothes pegs to hold them until the glue is dry.

Stack them on their sides and tie a belt round them to form a storage system or mail sorter.

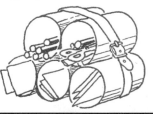

Polystyrene trays

To make a superglider, trace the patterns on the inside back cover on to paper and cut them out. Lay them on a clean, flat polystyrene tray. Cut out the shapes using a sharp knife (get help here). Decorate with stickers from the middle of this book. Push the wings and tailplane through the body. Slip a paper-clip over the nose of the plane to add weight. Adjust weight and bend down wing flaps to obtain a good flight.

Computer paper

The torn-off edges of continuous computer paper have their uses! If you know someone who uses this type of paper, ask them to save it for you.

You can make a useful supply of bookmarks for someone who works in a library or office. Cut the end off the cork from a wine bottle and stick it to a square of card with a hole at the top. Attach a bunch of computer paper edges on to the cork with a map pin through the end hole. Hang the bookmark holder where the user can reach out and pull one strip off when they need a marker.

THE RECYCLED HOME

I f we throw all our rubbish in the same bin it is impossible for it to be sorted and recycled. It is often thrown on to enormous rubbish tips which are then buried in the earth. But such methods are not the long-term answer. As the waste decays there is a danger that poisonous gases may build up and explode or catch fire. Poisons from the waste also wash down through the soil and pollute local water supplies. We are building up problems for ourselves. Yet if every family bothered to sort its own waste, most of the problems would be solved.

Many towns now have recycling centres, and by using these your family can dispose of its rubbish more usefully. Here are some ideas. Make sure your parents agree and are able to help you transport the things you collect to the local recycling centre. Also check which items the centre is prepared to take and how they should be packaged.

> **What do you call a frog who looks on the bright side?**
> *A hoptimist*

Getting started

Set aside a special area for your recycling efforts. Under the stairs, in the garage, in a basement or garden shed—anywhere that's dry and easily reached will do. Here you can store paper, tins, plastics, bottles, card and other items.

Paper

Find a strong cardboard box that will hold folded newspapers, cards and paper bags. Stand it on two wooden battens if the floor is damp. Make a short cut into each side with scissors and lay two pieces of string across the box. Tuck the ends into the cuts. When the box is full of paper, use the string to tie it firmly, ready for recycling. Replace the string and start again.

Cardboard

Cardboard can be stored and tied in the same way as paper. Make sure that it lies fairly flat by dismantling boxes, jumping on packets and tearing large pieces of cardboard in half.

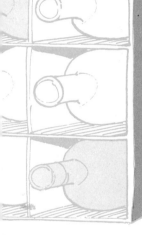

Plastics

Your local supermarket may accept some plastic drinks bottles for recycling. Collect these in another large cardboard box. The rest will still have to be thrown away with the rubbish, but you can reduce the room they take up by flattening them first.

Loosen the lid and stand on the bottle until all the air is forced out. Now tighten the lid and the bottle will stay flat.

Tins

tin-recycling kit consists of a orage bag, a wooden mallet, a agnet and an old sack.

At present, only non-magnetic, uminium cans may be recycled. s tins are emptied, test each one th the magnet. If the tin is tracted to the magnet it is not uminium and may be thrown vay. If it is not attracted, you ay recycle it, and it should first e washed and dried.

Then put each aluminium tin parately into the sack and eat it flat with the mallet. The ttened tins may be kept in the orage bag until you next visit the cycling centre.

Glass bottles

An old bottle crate makes a useful rack for storing and carrying glass. Most bottle banks like you to sort the bottles by colours and take off metal lids.

Clothes and stuff

Ask everyone in the house if they have anything they don't need. Good clothes and other odds and ends should be welcome at your local charity shop. Make sure each item is clean before you take it there. The rest can be folded and collected in a large black bin liner ready for the next jumble sale.

The rest

After all this recycling activity there should be very little rubbish left to throw away!

LITTER AND HOW TO BEAT IT

Many people drop their rubbish wherever they are, in the hope that someone else will clear it up. Because many of the things we buy are packaged in materials that do not rot away, we now have a problem with litter. This puts a massive strain on the local authority as well as making a mess of the cities and countryside.

Litter also creates many dangers. People and animals can be hurt by sharp edges, pavements are blocked, and disease-carrying creatures such as cockroaches and rats thrive.

If litter is a problem in your area, why not do something about it? Here are some ideas to get you going.

Get organized

You can't do everything yourself. In fact, it's more fun to get together in a group to tackle some things.

If you collect only a small amount of litter, you may be able to put it in your family's dustbins. Otherwise, look up the local cleansing service in the telephone book. It should come under your local council's services. Ask them where you are allowed to dump rubbish. Then plan how you will tidy up an area like your street, or a piece of waste ground.

You will need litterbusting equipment:

- ☛ Old clothes
- ☛ Gardening gloves
- ☛ Yard brooms
- ☛ Sacks and closures
- ☛ Pooper-scoopers (see page 3)
- ☛ Transport for the litter, such as an old buggy, pram base or wheelbarrow (or an old shopping bag)
- ☛ A paper-spear made from a long nail or knitting needle firmly taped to the end of an old broom handle
- ☛ Two large pieces of stiff card or hardboard for picking up leaves

Around your home

If everyone cleaned up the area around their own home, more than half the problem would be solved instantly. Maybe you and your family could set an example.

- ☛ Sweep the front path, pavement and gutter regularly.
- ☛ Make sure that you have enough dustbins for your own rubbish. Collect it in bags and close them securely. Check that your dustbin lids fit well and keep each lid in place with a brick in windy weather.

Why was the refuse collector sad?

Because he was down in the dumps

Litterbuster bag

Even if you hate to see litter in the street, it's not always easy to find a rubbish bin. That's where this great litterbuster bag comes in.

You will find the litterbuster hinge among the special stickers in the middle of this book. Fix one side of the hinge to the outside of a small plastic bag (at the top) and stick the other side to the inside of your school bag.

Put any unwanted rubbish into the plastic bag. When it's full, remove it from your school bag and use the hinge to seal it shut. Throw it away when you get home.

When you've used the sticker make your own hinges from self-sticking address labels.

ENERGY

Save your energy

You may not be able to do anything about energy policy nationally, but what about your own home? One third of all the energy we produce is used in the home, so if every family saved energy it would make a difference.

Use this check-list to see how your house rates. Then discuss it with the family and see how you can work together to improve the situation.

P = Problem   S = Solution

P Heat loss through roof.

☐ S Insulate loft floor.

P Heat lost from pipes and tank.

☐ S Lag both to keep heat in.

P Heat lost through windows.

☐ S Fit double glazing.

P Heat loss through walls.

☐ S Insulate cavity walls, line solid walls inside or outside.

P Draughts waste heat.

☐ S Draught-proof all round.

P Lights left on.

☐ S Turn off when not in use.

P Electric appliances left on.

☐ S Last person to use them should turn them off.

P Inefficient boiler.

☐ S Check and service regularly.

Cook-in-a-box

This idea relies on good insulation to conserve heat energy.

Line the inside and lid of a strong cardboard box with aluminium foil, shiny sides showing. Using material that conducts heat poorly—such as hay, straw, blankets or news-paper—make a 'nest' inside the box for a casserole dish with a tight-fitting lid.

Persuade whoever is cooking to prepare a casserole first thing in the morning. When it is thoroughly heated but not completely cooked, place the casserole, with the lid on, in your box. Cover it with an old blanket and put a heavy weight on the lid of the box.

The casserole will continue to cook in its own heat all day and by evening will be done to perfection!

Porridge is also delicious cooked in the box overnight.

Throughout most of history, people have needed very little energy to live. Wood for heating and cooking, oil or candle wax for lighting, horses for transport and food for our muscles to do the work were enough.

Then, in the West, came the Industrial Revolution, when people invented energy-driven machines to do many tasks. Ever since, we have been busy making things easier for ourselves. But there has been a cost: we have gradually been polluting our planet and over-using its natural resources.

We are now beginning to realize that, unless we plan carefully how to meet our energy needs in the future, there may be no future for us or our planet.

Fuel-savers

Paper Logs

If you use a log-burning stove or an open fire, this idea will help you save on fuel and recycle your waste paper at the same time.

Collect the cardboard tubes from toilet rolls and paper towels. Tear old newspapers into small pieces and soak them in a bucket of hot water overnight. When the paper is pulpy, shape it into balls by squeezing the water out. Stuff these tightly into the cardboard tubes. Wrap in a paper kitchen towel and leave in a warm place to dry. Your 'logs' can now be burned on the fire.

If you keep up a steady supply, this free, slow-burning fuel will save money.

ENERGY-SAVING ZONE

If you have an area of the house which is your own you may be able to use some of these ideas to make it an energy-saving zone.

Draught beaters

Before you can beat any cold draughts, you need to know where they're coming from. Find out using a small feather tied to a piece of cotton. Holding the cotton, suspend the feather near windows, the door or other possible draughty areas—it will move in the slightest breath of wind.

Stop draughts under your door with a long dog.

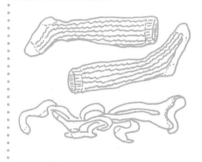

Stuff two long socks with clean old tights and sew them together in the middle.

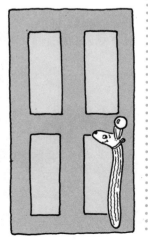

Tie a bow round one end to make a head, and embroider a face. Sew on two loops of ribbon for ears.

Place the dog along the bottom of your closed door to stop the draughts. When he's not in use, he can hang from the handle by his ears!

Make a caterpillar for draughty sash windows.

Measure the width of your window. Cut two strips of material to the same length and about 8cm wide.

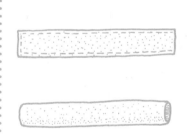

Ask someone to machine-stitch round three sides of the material, leaving one end open. Turn this long thin bag inside out. Half fill the bag with clean, dry sand and sew up the end.

Spread the sand flat inside and tie round with string at intervals, to stop the sand moving about too much. Decorate as a caterpillar. Place it along the middle of the window where the draught comes in.

Homework cosy

Keep warm while doing your homework by slipping into a sleeping bag before you sit down. Famous author Roald Dahl was rumoured to sit like this while writing in the winter.

Lighting

When a light bulb blows in your room, see if the family will invest in one of the new energy-saving light bulbs. They are more expensive than ordinary bulbs but consume 80 per cent less energy than a standard bulb and last eight times longer.

Check-list

Why not copy this list and put it on your bedroom door to remind you of different ways of saving energy, especially in winter? Every little helps!

YOU ARE NOW LEAVING AN ENERGY-SAVING ZONE

- ☐ Have you shut the windows?
- ☐ Have you closed the curtains?
- ☐ Have you switched off all appliances?
- ☐ Have you switched off the lights?
- ☐ Now close the door behind you

Energy facts

- ☞ More energy streams from the sun to the earth in a single day than the whole world uses in a year.

- ☞ Your body can exert only a few hundred watts of energy at a time. A small motor mower makes 2000 watts.

- ☞ Every day, each person in the USA uses about 30 times the amount of energy used by someone in a Third World country.

- ☞ Six thousand windmills, designed in 1460 by Venetian engineers, are still in daily use supplying power to work irrigation pumps for the island of Crete. That's good value!

- ☞ By the year 2000, one fifth of California's electricity will be generated by modern windmills.

- ☞ The most efficient form of lighting known to us is produced by the glow-worm. Unfortunately it cannot be put to any practical use!

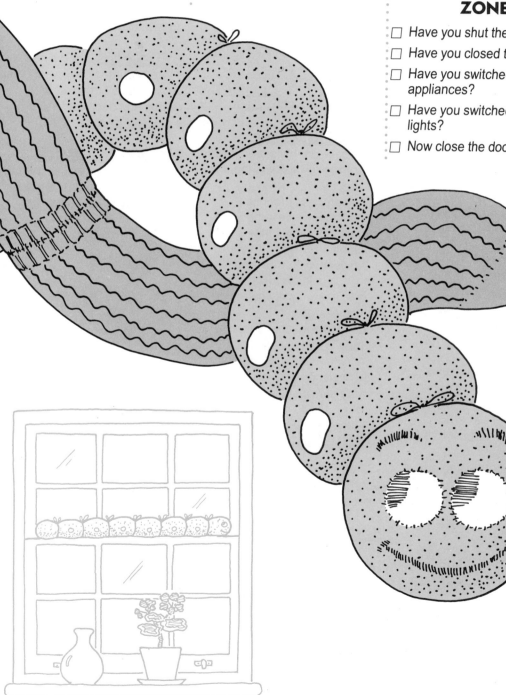
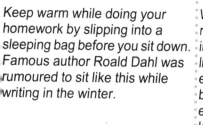

FUTURE ENERGY

Ever since we began to invent labour-saving machines, we have been using up energy in the form of fuel. But the earth's supply of fuels will not last for ever. In fact our main supplies of 'fossil fuels'—coal, oil, peat and gas—are running out fast. So the race is on to develop renewable fuel supplies such as hydroelectric and nuclear power. But these, too, have problems.

We need to develop alternative energy sources which are safer and less polluting. Only then can we be sure that we will not destroy the delicate balance of our world.

What kind of sweets kill forests?

Acid drops

Problems

COAL is one of the most polluting fuels to use, producing poisonous gases and contributing to acid rain.
It is dangerous to extract.
Mined land is often unusable afterwards and can be dangerous.
Supplies are running out.

GAS gives off poisonous fumes when it is burned.
The drilling process is very dangerous, with the risk of explosions.
Gas pipelines damage plant and animal habitats.
Supplies are running out.

OIL produces poisonous gas leading to acid rain when it is burned.
Oil spills at sea cause widespread destruction of fish, birds and seashore life.
Supplies are running out.

HYDROELECTRIC POWER is produced by harnessing the natural force of running water.
It can only be used in hilly areas where there is a good supply of water.
The damming of a river means disruption and loss of land.

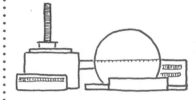

NUCLEAR POWER uses the enormous energy stored in atoms of uranium by splitting them apart in a reactor.
The process produces radioactive waste—the most lethal of all known man-made poisons.
Nuclear waste remains dangerous for thousands of years. It is difficult and expensive to dispose of.
Even low-level radiation is known to cause cancer.
Accidents at nuclear power stations can endanger people in a wide surrounding area.

Tomorrow's world

Safer and cleaner forms of energy production are being researched in many countries.

SOLAR POWER is harnessed by using reflectors and glass to trap energy from the sun's rays. It can be used to heat an individual house, or to heat steam which drives a turbine.

WIND POWER is making a comeback. Windmills are being used to generate electricity. In Denmark, for instance, the world's first offshore wind farm supplies over one tenth of the electricity needed by a town of 4,000 people.

THERMAL ENERGY is harnessed by using the heat deep inside the earth to heat steam to drive a turbine.

WAVE POWER is the newest energy source to be investigated using waves both in coastal waters and deep under the surface of the sea.

OTHER POSSIBILITIES include planting special fast-growing trees to meet a local community's fuel needs, and burning industrial waste.

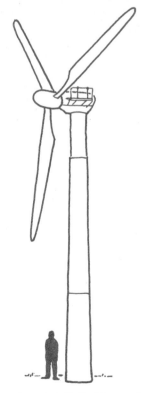

Huge modern windmills like this are called wind turbines. In some countries electricity is now being produced by hundreds of turbines on 'wind farms'.

SELF-SUFFICIENCY

A long time ago, people who worked their own land could live almost entirely on the things they grew and made themselves. This is called being self-sufficient. Today few people can live like that. Most of us are dependent on others to grow our food, make our clothes, provide us with lighting, heating, water and everything else we need. We, in our turn, work to earn money which we can then give for these goods and services.

There's nothing wrong with this system, provided we don't become totally incapable of doing things for ourselves! It's a good idea to use our own skills and abilities sometimes. Here are some examples.

Potions and lotions

Be a household chemist and make some 'home-grown' preparations for yourself or to give away. Take care, though. Chemicals can be dangerous. Only mix things you know are safe, and never taste anything you are not sure of.

☞ Make your own hair rinse. Warm water with vinegar works wonders on dark hair and lemon juice adds shine to blonde.

☞ A good pore-cleaning scrub can be made from a sticky mixture of oatmeal and honey, or sugar with olive oil. Make a small amount in a bowl and gently scrub your face with it. Rinse it off with plenty of water.

☞ Sunburn can be eased with natural yoghourt, applied with cotton wool.

☞ Treat tired television-eyes by lying down with two thin slices of cucumber on your closed eyelids.

☞ Make the family a pot of metal-cleaning paste. Mix 2 tablespoons of salt with enough vinegar to dissolve it. Add flour to make a fairly dry paste. Keep it in a plastic tub with a lid. Use a small amount on a cloth to clean brass, copper and pewter.

Stationery

☞ Keep Christmas and birthday cards. Tear off the backs to use for homework notes or telephone messages. Cut out the best pictures, punch a hole in the corner and thread with cotton to make gift tags.

☞ Do away with envelopes altogether. Write your letter on a plain piece of paper. Fold it in on itself four ways, fold the last corner over to the front and stick it down with the stamp.

Several of these ideas would make great presents.

TOYS AND GAMES

Perhaps it's just as well that very few of us can afford to buy all the expensive toys advertised on TV. It can be far more fun to invent and make things yourself. The best plan is to buy a few toys and then to make the accessories and special equipment they need.

All the examples given here are for toys that have been popular recently. By now there may well be something new in the shops, but you can follow the basic principles to make something really up to date.

Accessories

If you have some figures from one of the current sets of action toys, build them a headquarters to work from. You could base the model on a shop-bought one or invent your own.

Creepy Castle is made out of papier maché. Make this by putting small pieces of newspaper into a bowl of hot water and leaving them to soak overnight. Squeeze out as much of the water as possible. Pour in a cupful of wallpaper paste and mix with your hands until it is sticky.

Stand a shoebox on its end and tape the lid so that it makes an opening door. Mould the papier maché on to this frame. Allow it to dry in a warm place, before painting and varnishing.

Spooky Slime is made from two tablespoons cornflour mixed with two tablespoons cold water in a bowl. Add two drops of green food colouring.

The mixture feels very strange —hard when you squeeze it and runny when you stop! It is quite safe to use and easily washes off clothes.

Recycled toys

Not everything has to be bought new. Raid your local charity shop or a jumble sale for bargains. They will need a thorough wash, and may also need some mending and a coat of paint, but you can soon make them almost as good as new.

Why not make a collection of old toys (in good condition)? If they are no longer popular you can buy them for next to nothing and they may be collectors' items one day.

A **Space Command Head-quarters** would be great for an action figures. It is built from boxes and pieces of packaging stuck on to a large piece of cardboard and painted to look like buildings and space technology. Use some of the stickers from the middle of this book to make it look more convincing. Continue adding to the layout as you buy new toys.

SPACE COMMAND

DANGER

Dolls' world

Sindy, Barbie and similar toys have so many clothes and accessories that it is impossible to buy everything. Collect scraps of material, felt and fun fur and design a collection of clothes for your own dolls. You can make your own patterns by borrowing bought clothes, laying them flat and drawing round them.

A short skirt and sun top for a standard 30cm doll can be made using the patterns on the inside back cover. Draw over them using tracing paper, pin it on to your material and cut out. If sewing is difficult, ask a grown-up to sew the clothes for you.

Closures can be made from two tiny pieces of Velcro stuck to the fabric.

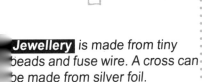

Jewellery is made from tiny beads and fuse wire. A cross can be made from silver foil.

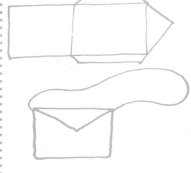

A handbag is made from fabric glued to a strip of folded card. The strap is a length of jewellery chain.

A toy multi-storey home can be built from polystyrene ceiling tiles, strengthened by sticking them to thin card. Decorate the inside with wrapping paper.

Furniture can be made using matchboxes and flexible drinking straws.

A table made with cardboard and straws.

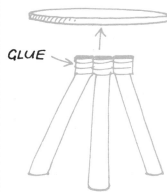

GLUE

A chair made with a matchbox and straws.

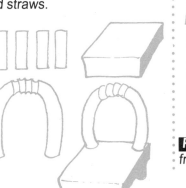

A sideboard made with four matchboxes, beads and covered in paper.

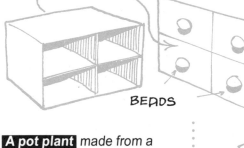

BEADS

A pot plant made from a toothpaste tube lid, wire and plasticene.

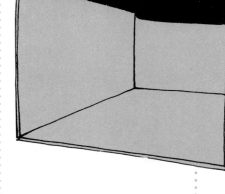

Pictures cut from magazines, framed in card.

FOOD TO SHARE

Cooking is always fun and sharing the end result with others makes it even better. Here are some ideas for the ecologically-minded cook.

Cooking can use up a lot of expensive energy. Why not have a no-cook meal once a week? It will save the cook's time, help you to keep healthy and save money.

NO-COOK MENU

Starters

GRAPEFRUIT
Cut in half. Cut round each segment and remove pips.

SARDINE PÂTÉ and RAW VEGETABLES
Drain and mash sardines from two tins with 25g butter, 100g cream cheese, a squirt of lemon juice, salt and pepper.
Cut vegetables such as raw carrots, red and green peppers and cucumber into strips to dip into the pâté.

Main course

COLD MEATS, TINNED FISH

GREEN SALAD, TOMATO and ONIONS, sliced SPRING ONIONS, OLIVES

BAKED BEANS

FRENCH BREAD or PITTA, CRISPS

CHEESES

DRIED FRUIT (such as SULTANAS, RAISINS and APRICOTS), NUTS

Desserts

GREEK YOGHOURT AND HONEY
Put a tablespoonful of creamy Greek-style yoghourt into a small bowl, sprinkle with honey and sesame seeds.

FRESH FRUIT

FROZEN BANANA
(Not strictly a no-cook dish, but this uses very little energy!) Cut a banana in half. Stick a lolly stick in one end, wrap in non pvc foodwrap and freeze. When frozen, remove the wrapping, dip the banana in melted chocolate and roll in chopped nuts.

Solar iced tea

Use the sun's power to make iced tea. Put two tea bags in a large glass jar of warm water. Stand it on a windowsill in the sun for seven to eight hours to brew. When it's a good colour, store it in the fridge until ready to serve with ice and lemon.

Fresh orange drink

Wash an orange and make a small hole in the top. Push a sugar lump into the hole. Hold the orange to your lips and squeeze the juice through the sugar lump. Delicious, but perhaps not for when visitors come to tea!

No-cook sweets

Crumble chocolate-cake crumbs in a bowl and mash with chocolate and hazelnut spread until you have a stiff dough. Roll into balls and coat with vermicell

CLOSE TO HOME

You may feel that you don't usually have a lot of say in the running of your home. All the decisions are made by adults. But you can still have an influence. Get everyone in your household involved in answering the questions in this light-hearted quiz. It may lead to some changes for the better.

Scoring

Give yourself 20 points for every B, 10 points for every A and 5 for each C.

If you scored 137 or over, well done! You obviously realize that caring for the environment begins at home. Between 82 and 136? You could do better. You're still sticking to some wasteful ways of doing things. How about a re-think? Less than 81? What slobs! Come on now, bully those adults into better ways before it's too late. If you scored 221—you cheated!

Green home?

Cleaning

What do your family use to clean the sink, bath and toilet:

☐ A. A full range of cleaners including bleach, scouring powder and water freshener

☐ B. Strong vinegar solution, a mixture of soda and soap in hot water and phosphate-free cleaners

☐ C. A quick wipe-round with a cloth?

How does your family dispose of dangerous chemicals, such as DIY cleaners, paint, car oil and battery acid:

☐ A. Put them straight down the outside drain

☐ B. Ring up the council's waste disposal department and put them where they suggest

☐ C. Never do any DIY?

What do your family keep in the bathroom:

☐ A. Something for every single need, i.e. shampoo, deodorant, bubble bath, perfume

☐ B. Only buy products with natural ingredients and try to use them sparingly

☐ C. Toothpaste and a bar of soap?

Food

Which would you rather your parents bought:

☐ A. Perfect, , mass-produced fruit and factory farmed eggs

☐ B. Organically grown fruit and free range eggs, even if they are a bit muddy and odd sizes

☐ C. A hamburger?

When your family buys tinned fruit, do you:

☐ A. Look for the biggest tin for the price

☐ B. Check the country of origin and list of contents carefully

☐ C. Grab the nearest?

Which would you rather eat:

☐ A. A pre-cooked, frozen steak pie and deep-fried chips

☐ B. A vegetarian lasagne you cooked yourself from fresh ingredients

☐ C. A takeaway hamburger?

Waste disposal

How do you get rid of your rubbish:

☐ A. Put it all in plastic sacks by the back gate

☐ B. Sort everything and take most of it down to the recycling plant, leaving a small amount to be bagged for collection

☐ C. Throw it over the fence?

Health

When you have a cold, do your parents:

☐ A. Buy every cure on the market and hope something works

☐ B. Avoid drugs if possible, only taking them on prescription from a doctor. Go for prevention rather than cure

☐ C. Take paracetamol and hope for the best?

Furnishings

Would you rather have:

☐ A. Smart mass-produced furniture using new materials

☐ B. Furniture, old or new, made with natural materials such as wood, cane and cotton

☐ C. Anything, as long as it's cheap?

In the garden

When planning the garden did your family:

☐ A. Go for convenience, with paving stones, potted plants, chemical fertilizers and pesticides

☐ B. Prefer a balanced chemical-free garden with room for wildlife

☐ C. Not get around to it?

The car

When buying the car did your family:

☐ A. Go for performance and looks

☐ B. Prefer safety, low-pollution and economy

☐ C. Buy it from a friend?

YOUR OWN ROOM

Furniture

Many of our furnishings use up vast quantities of the earth's resources. Because of this, there is now a movement towards 'low tech'—reusing materials to make workable fun alternatives for our homes. Here are some examples of low tech furniture that you could use in your own room.

The way you look after your own space in the house gives a good picture of what you are like and the things you find important. Look at your own room. What does it say about you?

If you'd like it to be a Green Zone (you'll find a sticker for your door in the middle of this book), here are some ideas to get you started.

Decorating

Maybe you still have Mickey Mouse on your bedroom wallpaper and think it's time for a change. Redecorating your own room can be fun.

Get permission first, by preparing careful plans and drawings of what you would like to do. If your parents know you have thought about it, they may well be prepared to join in and help.

The hardest part of home decorating is the preparation. Ask someone to help you remove old wallpaper and fill any cracks in the plaster.

Wallpaper is expensive. Plain lining paper (which is often recycled), painted or stencilled, can look just as good.

You could recycle your favourite comics or magazines by using them as wallpaper. You will need a big collection to choose from. Decide on an overall colour scheme for the room and then select magazine pages featuring those colours. It is best to treat only one wall in this way and to paint the others a plain colour.

Prepare the walls and line with plain ceiling paper. Brush wallpaper paste over a small area and begin sticking interesting pages to the wall to form a kind of patchwork. When the whole area is covered, allow it to dry and then add a coat of size (from a DIY shop) to seal it.

Seating

Chairs made from inflated car or truck tyre inner tubes. Place a large square of fabric on the floor and stack the inner tube(s) on it. Pull up the corners of the fabric, tie opposites together in a knot and tuck them inside the tube(s).

If using more than one tube, tie a piece of cord around the outside, between the tubes, to tighten the fabric and keep them together.

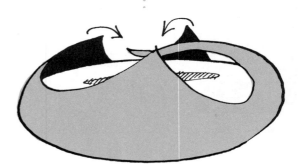

LITTERBUSTER

BAG HINGE

GREAT LITTERBUSTER PLAN P.6

Save energy: stay in bed!

IT'S NOT EASY BEING GREEN

THIS IS A GREEN ZONE

SEE P. 16

DANGER

KEEP OUT

TXR VII

KJX 94A

LRD 179

HIGH VOLTAGE

SPACE COMMAND

PRIVATE

FLASHES FOR SPACE COMMAND HEADQUARTERS P.12

SUPER GLIDER P. 3

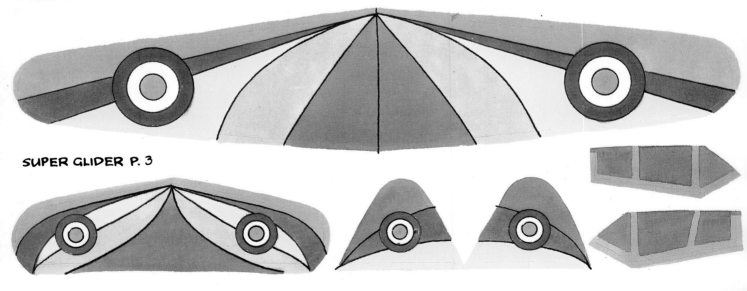

Scatter cushions are easy to make from oddments of material. They can be filled with old tights and tee shirts.

Sag bags or large cushion seats look good made from woven sacks. You can usually ask for these at bakeries, breweries or restaurants who buy materials in bulk. Wash them carefully and stuff with an old eiderdown folded into four and sewn together at the corners.

Another useful filling is the polystyrene pellets used to package hi-fi equipment. These are often thrown away outside shops. They are so light they can be impossible to recapture if they blow about, so take them home in their box and pour them carefully into your sack.

with rawl plugs and screws.

Storage can be hung on the wall by making a grid of wooden battens. Nail as many as you like to two cross bars and ask for help

to attach the whole thing to your wall. Tins and plastic tubs can be hung directly on to screws driven half way into the wood.

Old jeans pockets can be tacked on to a piece of plywood to make a decorative storage unit.

Use the undersides of your shelves by making a hole in the metal lids of screw-top glass jars and attaching them under the shelf. The jars can then be screwed into the lids and hang suspended.

Notice board

A bulletin board looking like an enormous clipboard is made from a large piece of pinboard (from your timber merchant or DIY shop) covered with a length of green baize material. Staple the fabric on the back of the board so that it is smooth on the front.

To make the clip, cut the middle portion from a fizzy drinks bottle. Make two slits in the plastic as shown. Cut two clip shapes the same length as the plastic from stiff card and cover them with silver foil. Push them through the slots and on to the top of the board.

Lampshades

A cheese grater or salad shaker makes a good and original small lampshade. You will need someone to drill a hole for the flex.

Storage

A clothes rail for your coats and hats can be made from round wooden door handles screwed into a short batten. Ask someone to help you attach it to the wall

IN THE GARDEN

Not everyone has a large garden, but that need not stop you being interested in growing things.

Just a windowsill

If the only outdoor space you have is a windowsill or balcony, you can still grow something at almost any time of year.

☞ *A wallpaper-hanging tray from a DIY shop makes a good windowbox. Punch holes in the bottom, stand it on pieces of wood and fill it with seed compost.*

For a herb garden, plant parsley, radish, mint and spring onions. You might also try basil, sage and thyme.

☞ *An unusual and space-saving idea is to grow your herbs and pot plants in a hanging garden made from an old birdcage. Make sure you wash the cage thoroughly before putting any pots in it.*

Who's green and lies very still?

Kermit the Log

Indoor gardening

☞ *Grow mustard and cress on damp cotton wool in a margarine tub. When it reaches 7cm cut it, wash off any seeds and eat it in sandwiches or with salad.*

☞ *Sprout mung beans, alfalfa and cress seeds in a jam jar. Soak the beans in water overnight. Cover the open end with a piece of material and secure with an elastic band. Turn it over so that the water strains out and leave on a saucer in a dark place overnight. Once a day, wash the beans, drain them and put them back. After a few days they will be ready to eat—a rich source of vitamin C and good in salads and sandwiches.*

Compost

Teach the family to recycle anything that will rot down into compost. You will save bin space and improve the soil in your garden.

☞ *Place a large plastic tub with a lid in the kitchen for tea bags, potato peelings, and any left-over food (except meat scraps).*

Build a simple frame from bricks, wood and planks or chicken wire supported by stakes. If you have room

prepare two compost containers. It will be about six months before the first one is ready, so it's useful to have another to fill while you are waiting.

Put a layer of sticks on the bottom to help air circulate underneath. Then add layers of garden rubbish, kitchen waste, special nitrogen 'activator' bought from a garden shop and finally a layer of soil. Repeat these layers until the heap is full. Moisten it by sprinkling with water.

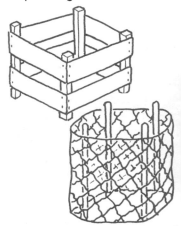

When the frame is nearly full, cover the heap with a plastic bin liner to keep the heat in and leave it for six months. When it's ready, take away the frame and dig the compost into your vegetable patch or flower beds.

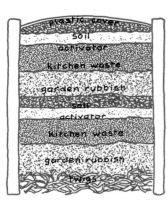

SUPERSHOPPER

Today most people buy their food rather than producing it for themselves. A quick look along the shelves at the local supermarket shows that this comes from all over the world and we now have food choices that would have been unheard-of only a few years ago. This is good, as a varied diet is healthy. But we should think before buying our food, making sure we are happy about where it comes from and how it is packaged and manufactured.

The more you know about household shopping, the more helpful you can be when your family goes to the supermarket. You can check labels, examine the produce and find the best value—all things that the busy shopper never has time to do. There are all sorts of things to look out for if you want to be a supershopper.

Clean and safe?

Things to look out for:
- Check that food counters, the shelves and shop floor are clean.
- Check each sell-by date. If it has passed, the product is no longer fresh.
- Look out for safe tamper-proof seals.
- Buy medicines and household cleaners with child-proof lids.

Exploitation

Sometimes food production causes hardship and even cruelty to both people and animals. You may wish to avoid buying:
- Fish from countries whose fishermen hunt rare species of whale.
- Beef products from South America, where the rain forests are being cut down to make room for cattle ranches.
- Veal, because this meat comes from calves reared in restrictive conditions.
- Rennet, used to make cheese, comes from the stomachs of unweaned calves. There is an alternative called Mucor miehei.
- Eggs laid by 'battery' hens living in cramped conditions. Buy 'free range' eggs instead.
- Products from countries where people are seriously discriminated against on the grounds of colour, class or religion.

Environment

- Never buy aerosol sprays that can destroy the ozone layer around the earth. Choose ozone-safe brands, or a spray bottle with a trigger.
- Suggest that your family uses pot-pourri instead of chemical room fresheners.
- Buy unbleached white toilet paper and kitchen towels made from recycled paper. The dye from coloured rolls can pollute rivers.

Health

For a healthy diet remember the following things:
- Organically-grown vegetables and fruits—produced without chemical fertilizers or insecticides—are better for you.
- Saturated fat can contribute to heart disease. Buy low-fat margarine; oil made from olives, sunflowers or vegetables; and canned fish in brine.
- Cut down on sugar. Buy fewer sweets and tinned fruit in natural juice rather than syrup.
- Cut down on salt.
- High-fibre, wholemeal breads are best for you.

Additives

- Read the contents list on packaged food. Avoid goods with lots of extra ingredients, such as emulsifiers, preservatives and artificial colours.
- Try to buy environment-friendly cleaning materials. Don't buy those containing phosphates, bleaches, whiteners and enzymes that will be flushed into the water system and damage the environment.

At the check-out

- Try to buy products which use little packaging.
- Ask for paper bags rather than plastic.
- Reuse carrier bags or take a basket when you shop.

ADDING VALUE

In some countries people have to pay VAT—Value Added Tax. The government collects extra money on any raw material that has been processed to increase its value. You can do a bit of value-adding and transform inexpensive items from high street shops into useful items for yourself or gifts for others. You'll find lots of ideas on the next few pages.

The DIY centre

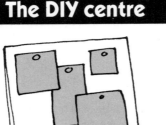

☞ Cork floor tiles make good mini bulletin boards. Cut one into a special shape and use it to hold badges or pins.

FELT

☞ Ceramic tiles make great stands for teapots or hot saucepans. Buy a nice one and stick a piece of felt on the base to prevent scratching a table or work surface.

Jewellery

Nearly anything can and is being used by today's top jewellery designers. Why not make some original jewellery of your own?

☞ Copper rings used in plumbing can look good. Make sure they have no sharp edges. Give them with a coat of clear varnish. to keep them bright.
☞ Wool, ribbon or plastic-covered wire can be plaited into friendship bracelets.
☞ Big wooden curtain rings, painted and varnished, make lovely bangles for small wrists.
☞ Pasta and seeds can be threaded and painted.
☞ Copper wire can be made into chains, or a name brooch.

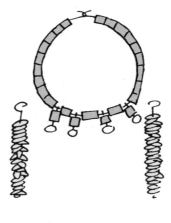

The sweetshop

☞ The big plastic jars you see in sweetshops make good storage jars. Ask the shopkeeper if you can have a few old ones. Wash them, soak off the labels and add your own.
☞ Buy a few sweets as a present for someone. Use this pattern to make a special box to put them in.

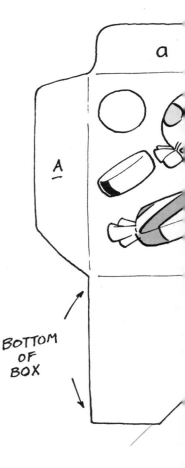

a

A

BOTTOM
OF
BOX

Trace the shape below on to a piece of thin card and colour in the design with felt-tipped pens or crayons. Cut it out and score along the dotted lines.

Glue flap A to the inside of the box at B. Fold in the two smaller bottom flaps, then overlap the larger ones and glue together. Fold over the top flaps a, b and c

and tuck them into each other. Fold along the dotted line marked C and tuck flap d into the lid. This makes a built-in gift tag!

MORE VALUE ADDED

H ere are more simple and fun ways for you to put everyday household items to a completely new use. Why not see what other ideas you can think of?

The hardware store

☛ Make a smart Chinese-style food warmer to keep your next takeaway meal hot. Buy a cheap baking tray about 4cm deep. Attach four night-lights inside it with sticky putty and cover it with a cake rack.

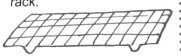

☛ In many countries, there is a long tradition of making dolls from round wooden clothes pegs.

☛ Painted and decorated pegs can be used to clip cards to a length of string for a birthday or Christmas display.

☛ Spring-type pegs can also be used to make models or dolls' furniture. Models made from wooden pegs (see below) look great painted and varnished. Why not make a peg monster like the one below?

☛ Plastic-coated garden wire can be cut and twisted with pliers to make all kinds of models and toys. This wonderful wire horse and cart was made by a boy in Zimbabwe.

OUT AND ABOUT

It's easy to get gloomy about the future when you look at all the things we've been doing to pollute and ruin the beautiful world God gave us. But a visit to the country or a local park will remind you that nature is strong and capable of adapting to change in a remarkable way. The world is not totally ruined, and people are now more aware of the need to take care of what we have been given. The more we know about the world, the more we'll care for it and do our best to protect it. So let's get going!

Know your area

You may have been born and brought up in one area so that you take your surroundings for granted, missing out on the surprises they have to offer. If so, now's the time to take a new look.

Start at your local library or planning offices. They usually have large-scale maps that you can photocopy. Mark out an area of about a mile around your home, noting parks, cemeteries, ponds, rivers or waste ground where wildlife could flourish.

Explore each place, making notes and rough drawings of everything you see. When you get home, plot these on the map.

You may find a conservation group at work somewhere in your neighbourhood or community. They will be able to check your findings against their own and tell you what is happening locally.

Nature detective

Look out for the tiny clues left by all living creatures.

Tracks left in muddy ground

Dog

Fox

Squirrel

Rat

Mouse

Rabbit

Other clues to look for

Acorns bitten by squirrel

Nuts opened by vole or mouse

Snails smashed by thrush

Bark eaten by deer

Sheep's wool on barbed wire

Deer and rabbit droppings

ENJOYING NATURE

There's something about being out in the countryside, in a park or by a large lake or the sea that makes people feel happy to be alive. Perhaps being close to nature reminds us what a big place the world is and how small we are, or it helps us get away from the everyday rush of home and school. Whatever the reason, it is great to spend time 'away from it all'.

There are many ways of enjoying the great outdoors. Walking, cycling, swimming, sailing and picnicking are all good—especially if you can do them with friends or family.

On these pages you will find some ideas for other things you might do to enjoy your surroundings.

Group games

Find It This can be played with any number of people. The leader tells all the players the name of a natural object they have to find. It could be a pine cone, a yellow leaf, or a bird's feather, depending on the area and time of year. The first one back with the correct object gains a point or takes over as leader.

Challenge Give the group a task, such as damming a stream or building a picnic table, using only natural objects. (Make sure to dismantle the dam and leave things just as you found them when you leave.)

Blind Nature Trail This encourages people to explore the sounds, smells and feel of an area.

Walk round beforehand with a ball of string, attaching it to trees, rocks, fences and any other interesting objects. Tie a knot in the string where there is something to explore, such as a hollow log or a clump of sweet-smelling flowers.

Collections

Making a collection is a great way of learning all about a subject that interests you. If you display your collection, other people can enjoy it too.

There is practically no limit to the things you might collect, but never pick rare wild flowers and make sure you do not disturb living things by pulling up the roots of plants, or gathering seashells or birds' eggs that contain living creatures.

Equipment This need not be expensive. You will need a good reference book, a notebook and pencil, collecting bag and storage boxes. When studying the objects you have found, you may need a bright light, a good magnifying glass (10x magnification), tweezers and a desk or table to work on.

Field notes Make a record in your notebook when you find something interesting. Write down the date, time and place, together with the object's name if you know it. At the same time, tie or stick a label to the object itself. Later you could keep the information in a card index or on computer.

Display Arranging your collection so that other people can look at it will add to your own pleasure. Photographs, pressed grasses or other flat objects can be pasted on to coloured paper to go on your wall or put into scrap books.

Small items such as shells or bones can be kept in cotton wool-lined matchboxes or the plastic drawers designed for storing screws and nails. If you have a cupboard with glass doors or some shelves, you could keep a whole museum of found objects.

More ideas for collections:
- Rocks
- Fossils
- Animal skulls or teeth
- Leaves
- Fungi
- Mosses and lichens
- Crystals
- Feathers

Recording nature

Photography is an excellent way to record what you see without disturbing it.

Your camera need not be elaborate. With practice you can get some good shots with a very ordinary camera using film with an ASA rating of 25-100 for bright light or 200-400 for poor light and close-up work. Colour prints are probably best to begin with.

To get a good close-up of an animal or bird, without using special lenses, hide behind a tree stump or fence post, resting your camera on the top to steady it. Wait patiently for the subject to move near you before taking a photograph.

Alternatively, you could creep up on your subject, making sure the wind is blowing towards you (so that the animal does not pick up your scent). Then lie on your stomach, steady the camera and shoot.

A panoramic picture can be created from a series of overlapping photographs. Take one picture, advance the film, then move the camera slightly to one side and take a second picture. Repeat this process several times, making sure each shot is taken at the same level.

Sound recordings

Recording the night sounds of animals, the birds' dawn chorus or individual bird songs can be exciting.

An ordinary cassette recorder works well, but it is best to have one with a digital counter and manual recording-level controls.

Use rechargeable or cadmium- and mercury-free batteries, which are better for the environment.

Get into position as quietly as possible and start each recording by speaking the date, location, weather and any other comments quietly into the microphone. Write the number showing on the recorder counter in a notebook, together with any other important details. Keep the machine in recording mode and use the pause button to start and stop.

Most recorders have built-in microphones which are fine for general use. But if you are buying one, a uni-directional (or cardioid) microphone is most useful for this type of work.

To avoid the noise of your finger movements, tape the micro-phone to a stick placed in the ground. An extension lead will help you set the microphone at a distance if you want to record wildlife without disturbing it.

Blindfold each person and start them off holding the string with one hand and exploring with the other. Encourage them to use all their senses (except sight).

When the game is over, your friends can go round the course again without the blindfold and see how much they remember.

Earth Windows This is a quiet game to be played in open woodland. (First make sure the ground is dry and no one is afraid of creepy-crawlies.)

Everyone lies down on the ground and the leader covers them with leaves, twigs and pine needles until only each person's face is showing. See who can stay like this the longest, watching everything that goes on from a completely new angle. You may be surprised by what you see, smell and feel!

YOUR OWN BACK YARD

We may not be able to change the world overnight, but each one of us can do something to begin the vital process locally.

Here are a few practical projects for you and your family, so that next time somebody says 'but what can we do?' you can give some useful suggestions.

'Green' Watch

As part of your survey of the area, use these simple tests to monitor pollution levels:

☞ Hold a thin cotton handkerchief over your mouth and breathe in steadily. Take it away and look at the area that was over your mouth. How clean is it?

☞ Collect 2.5cm rainwater through a tea strainer placed over a glass jar. Dip a strip of litmus paper (sold for chemistry sets) into the rainwater. If the colour changes to pinky purple, damaging acid is present in the rain.

☞ Look for lichens growing on trees, rocks or bricks. They can give you valuable clues because only some kinds can grow in polluted air.

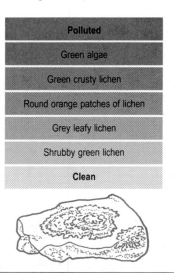

Polluted
Green algae
Green crusty lichen
Round orange patches of lichen
Grey leafy lichen
Shrubby green lichen
Clean

Action!

☞ Ask your local authority to see what they can do about reducing pollution from nearby factories.

☞ Encourage your family to walk, ride bicycles or use public transport .

☞ If your family runs a car, see if you can change to unleaded petrol or fit a catalytic converter which can reduce exhaust pollution by 90%.

☞ Avoid burning garden waste, or rubbish containing plastic, rubber or chemicals.

☞ Do not use harmful garden pesticides.

Wildlife

If you have any open space around your home, think about how you can make it welcoming to wildlife.

☞ Ask your parents if you can leave a small uncultivated area in the garden. Let the grass grow freely and allow wild flowers to self-seed. Michaelmas daisy, ragwort, vetch and nettles will grow easily and attract butterflies and other insects. These in turn will bring birds and small mammals into your garden. Provide them with drinking water in an old tray or dustbin lid sunk into the ground.

☞ Plant tubs can be made from car tyres painted white, wooden barrels cut in half, or old chimney pots with flower pots in the top.

☞ Paint pots or buckets make good hanging planters. Some water needs to collect in the bottom, but drainage holes in the side are important. Get help to drill these a little way above the base of your container.

☞ Even your own bedroom windowsill can be a welcoming feeding place for birds (make sure no cats can get on to it). Wedge a stick between the bricks on either side and hang it with half coconuts, bits of bacon fat, nuts or pine cones with melted fat in them.

Put out a heavy, shallow dish of water. The birds will soon get used to you watching from indoors and will look forward to this food in winter.

WORLDWIDE

On a world scale there is good news and there is bad news. The bad news is that, despite having been on this planet for a relatively short time, people have made massive environmental changes without fully realizing the way their actions affect the world as a whole. Now, we even have the power to destroy the earth with nuclear weapons. For the first time, the future is in doubt.

The good news is that, after several shock reports in the 1960s, people finally began to think about what we were doing to our planet. They formed the first of the groups that are now part of the 'green' movement and they have gradually been affecting the way people think and act. If they continue to inform and involve others, it may not be too late to save our world and its peoples.

Timescale

Planet earth is thought by some to be about 4,600 million years old. If we drop a few noughts and imagine that the earth is just 46 years of age, then its life story goes something like this.

The early years

Age 1–7
Nothing known

Age 7–42
Little known about the growing years

Age 42–45
Living things created

Last year

Age 45
Dinosaurs lived

Mammals created 8 months ago

This year

Age 46
The Ice Age happened at the weekend

Humankind around from about 4 hours ago

People discovered agriculture an hour ago

The Industrial Revolution happened a minute ago

We have made a rubbish tip of the planet in only the last 60 seconds!

Greenpeace

Members of Greenpeace believe in peaceful but direct action to defend the environment. They oppose nuclear power and weapons, pollution and the dumping of nuclear waste, the plundering of Antarctica and the killing of endangered species, especially the whale.

Friends of the Earth

Friends of the Earth campaigns for protection of wildlife and habitats, and for improvement of the environment at local, national and international levels.

WWF

The World Wide Fund for Nature campaigns for the conservation of wildlife and their habitats and the proper use of the earth's natural resources.

You will find the addresses of these and other 'green' organizations on page 32.

Green politics

Supporters of the 'green' movement have begun to get involved in politics so that their ideas and policies can be discussed and developed at a national level. They hope that by making large-scale changes to laws that affect the environment they may begin to solve some of the worst problems.

What do you call a mad conservationist?
Environ-mental

GLOBAL VILLAGE GAME

Satellites can send telephone, radio and television messages around the whole earth in a few seconds, so people can know what's happening on the other side of the world almost straight away. This has led to the world being called a 'global village'. As inhabitants of this village, we need to see and understand the whole picture if we are to do anything about it in our own corner.

This game (for three to seven players) will help you get a better picture of some of the world's environmental problems, their causes and effects, and the solutions needed. First paste a photocopy of these two pages on to a piece of thin card. Colour the cards with crayons or felt-tipped pens, as shown on the colouring guide on page 29. You could then cover them with clear adhesive plastic film for protection. Cut out the cards, shuffle them and the game is ready to play.

Play

The object of the game is to collect as many sets of three cards as possible.

Deal out all the cards to the players.

Player one, on the dealer's left, asks someone if he has a card she wants to collect, by asking a question like, 'Do you know the solution to the problem of acid rain?'

If that player has the solution card in the acid rain set, he reads out the answer and then hands it over to player one. If he does not hold the card, he answers 'no' and play passes to him.

When a player has three cards from one set he or she places them on the table.

When three people are playing, the game ends when one player runs out of cards. Otherwise the game continues until all the sets are completed. The person with the most complete sets of cards is the winner.

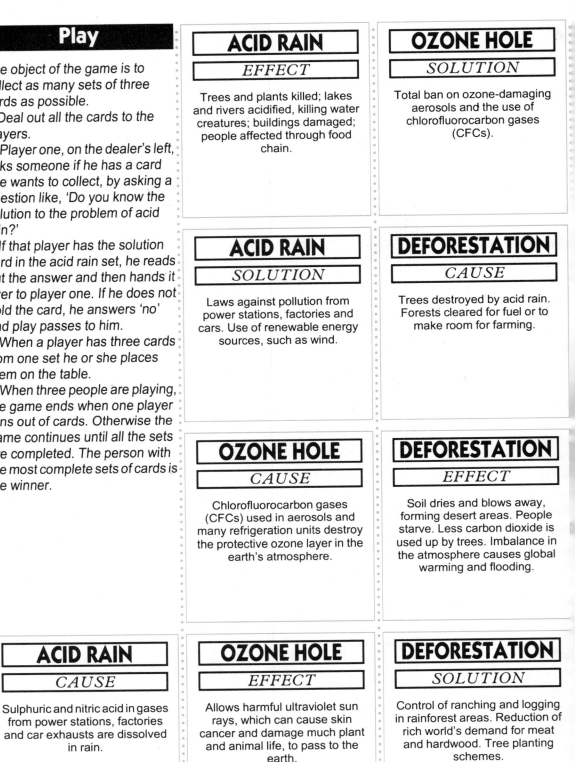

ACID RAIN — *EFFECT*
Trees and plants killed; lakes and rivers acidified, killing water creatures; buildings damaged; people affected through food chain.

OZONE HOLE — *SOLUTION*
Total ban on ozone-damaging aerosols and the use of chlorofluorocarbon gases (CFCs).

ACID RAIN — *SOLUTION*
Laws against pollution from power stations, factories and cars. Use of renewable energy sources, such as wind.

DEFORESTATION — *CAUSE*
Trees destroyed by acid rain. Forests cleared for fuel or to make room for farming.

OZONE HOLE — *CAUSE*
Chlorofluorocarbon gases (CFCs) used in aerosols and many refrigeration units destroy the protective ozone layer in the earth's atmosphere.

DEFORESTATION — *EFFECT*
Soil dries and blows away, forming desert areas. People starve. Less carbon dioxide is used up by trees. Imbalance in the atmosphere causes global warming and flooding.

ACID RAIN — *CAUSE*
Sulphuric and nitric acid in gases from power stations, factories and car exhausts are dissolved in rain.

OZONE HOLE — *EFFECT*
Allows harmful ultraviolet sun rays, which can cause skin cancer and damage much plant and animal life, to pass to the earth.

DEFORESTATION — *SOLUTION*
Control of ranching and logging in rainforest areas. Reduction of rich world's demand for meat and hardwood. Tree planting schemes.

What did the frog think of the book on wildlife? *Absolutely ribbeting*

WILDLIFE

WILDLIFE IN DANGER
CAUSE
Destruction of forest for more farmland. Careless use of pesticides in farming. Trade in luxury goods such as fur coats and ivory. Trade in exotic animals.

DESTRUCTIVE FARMING METHODS
EFFECT
Chemicals from artificial fertilizers and pesticides remain on food and seep into water supplies. Wildlife is destroyed. Animals suffer. Risk of food contamination increases.

NUCLEAR POLLUTION
SOLUTION
Use of other, renewable energy sources. Global ban on weapons testing (particularly above ground). International controls on safety in nuclear power industry, waste dumping and dismantling old power stations. World peace.

Colouring guide
Colour all 'CAUSE' panels......... pale blue
Colour all 'EFFECT' panels....... pale green
Colour all 'SOLUTION' panels........... pink
Colour all 'ACID RAIN' boxes............. red
Colour all 'OZONE HOLE' boxes ..... orange
Colour all 'DEFORESTATION' boxes . yellow
Colour all 'WILDLIFE...' boxes .... green
Colour all 'DESTRUCTIVE...' boxes..... blue
Colour all 'NUCLEAR...' boxes .... purple
Colour all 'WASTE OF...' boxes .... grey

WILDLIFE IN DANGER
EFFECT
Animals suffer loss of habitats. Extinction of species. Food chain is broken. Fewer resources for research into new drugs from plants.

DESTRUCTIVE FARMING METHODS
SOLUTION
Controls on land use and overproduction of foodstuffs. Longer-term approach to farming. Use of organic fertilizers and pesticides. Enforcement of laws on farming.

WASTE OF RESOURCES
CAUSE
Using natural resources with no thought for their renewal. Short-term planning motivated by the search for quick profits. Wastefulness and a throwaway mentality.

WILDLIFE IN DANGER
SOLUTION
International controls on destruction of habitats. Tougher laws on trading in animals and their products. Provision of game reserves, wildlife parks and gardens.

NUCLEAR POLLUTION
CAUSE
Testing and stockpiling of nuclear weapons. Contamination from nuclear fuel. Transporting and dumping nuclear waste. Dismantling of old nuclear power stations. Accidents.

WASTE OF RESOURCES
EFFECT
Natural resources in danger of running out completely. Destruction of natural balances. Poverty and a poorer lifestyle for everyone in the future.

DESTRUCTIVE FARMING METHODS
CAUSE
Demand for more and 'better' food products. Larger profits, speed and efficiency given priority over animal welfare.

NUCLEAR POLLUTION
EFFECT
Danger to the planet from accidents like that at Chernobyl in the USSR. Contamination from power stations. Pollution of the seas and death of marine life.

WASTE OF RESOURCES
SOLUTION
Recycling, especially of essential minerals. Emphasis on building things to last and repairing them, not throwing them away. More research into renewable materials.

☛ So many of these problems are caused by human greed. We want to use up the planet's resources for our own gain, here and now. This is not the way God planned for us to look after and conserve his beautiful creation. You can read more about this right at the beginning of the Bible where it says that it is our responsibility on earth 'to work it and take care of it' (Genesis 2:15).

GET INVOLVED

The national and international organizations trying to do something about the world's problems will succeed only if they have plenty of active supporters backing up their beliefs by giving time and money. Many organizations encourage family membership and also encourage people to get together in local groups.

Children sometimes think that they are powerless, unable to influence things that they feel strongly about. But don't underestimate yourself. A single person caring enough about something may mobilize a whole school, including the teachers. The power of a committed group is considerable.

Here are some practical ways in which you might get involved in the green revolution.

A green group

See if you can get a group together from friends at your school, church or youth club. If they are interested in one particular green organization, you could all join and work for it locally.

If your small group is enthusiastic, you could hold a larger meeting and involve more people.

To do this, you need to find somewhere to meet. Agree on a time and advertise the meeting with some interesting posters or handbills. The poster on the inside front cover of this book may be helpful here. Take photocopies of it, fill them in, and get your group to colour them.

Prepare for the meeting carefully. Agree wo should lead it, and ask someone to be the official note-taker. Have a written list of the things you want to discuss and work through it point by point. The last item on this list should be 'any other business'. This gives people a chance to add their own topics.

At the meeting, discuss your chosen project fully, decide the first steps to take and what each group member should do. Then set a date for the next meeting when people can report back.

Fund raising

Almost anything you try to do will involve spending money. The ability to raise your own finances is very useful.

The key to both giving and collecting money is making sure that people enjoy themselves while doing it. That way, everyone will want to join in. Here are some money-raising ideas for you to try. First, make sure your parents agree with your plans.

☞ **Sponsorship** Decide on a really difficult or intriguing task such as not watching the TV for a week. Tell everyone what you are going to attempt and ask them to give you a sum of money, or so much an hour, if you succeed. Write down their promise and ask them to sign it. Collect the money when you have completed the task.

☞ **Selling things** Decide what you have to sell and where you could sell it. For example, you could sort out your old toys and sell them in the playground at lunch break (with permission). Or you might provide refreshments at a school sports match by baking biscuits or making popcorn.

☞ **Entertaining** If you have lots of talent in your group, offer to put on a revue at the end of term. Make sure you have a good mix of 'acts' and perhaps persuade a local personality to be the star attraction. All the ticket money can go to your project.

Wordsearch

the following words are hidden the sunflower. You may find em written forwards, ckwards or diagonally. We ve marked 'OZONE' for you as example. How many can you d?

ACID RAIN
OZONE
GREEN
HABITAT
POLLUTION
RECYCLING
LITTER
LICHEN
OCEAN
SEA
SKY
RAIN
SUN
CYCLE
NATURE

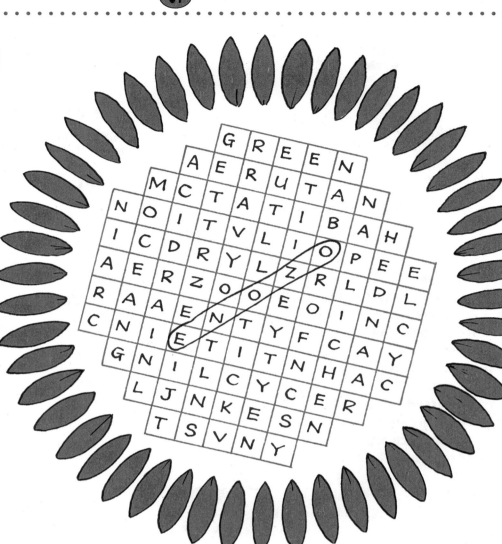

he sunflower is one of the ages used by the green ovement. It represents growth into a better and more autiful world.

preading the word

ere are many opportunities to people what you have learned out the way we are treating the rld. You could speak to your ss, to a group at church or to y clubs you belong to. At school u could take an assembly, or ange a debate or a meeting h an invited speaker. You ght even be able to take part in ervice at a local church. any of the organizations listed page 32 have information flets and resource sheets to lp you spread the word about portant green issues. You might also like to read or

think about some of the following poems and prayers:

Keep in your heart
a green bough
And God will send you
a singing bird.

Celtic prayer

A tree which moves some to
tears of joy is in the eyes of
others only a green thing
which stands in the way.

William Blake

Not a creature is lost,
Not a feather is torn,
But God in his heaven
Will see it and mourn.

Anon

The heavens declare
the glory of God;
the skies proclaim
the work of his hands.
Day after day
they pour forth speech;
night after night
they display knowledge.
There is no speech or
language where their
voice is not heard.

Psalm 95:1-4

Praised be my Lord
for our sister water,
who is very
serviceable
unto us and humble
and precious and
clean.

Francis of Assisi

Blessèd art thou,
O Lord our God,
King of the Universe,
who bringest forth
food from the earth.

A Jewish grace

Useful addresses

Here are some addresses of organizations that will be able to give you further information about a range of environmental and conservation issues. If you write, enclose a stamped addressed envelope and make sure you have explained clearly what you need to know.

British Trust for Conservation Volunteers

36 St Mary's Street
Wallingford
Oxfordshire OX10 0EU

Friends of the Earth

26-28 Underwood Street
London N1 7JQ

Greenpeace

30-31 Islington Green
London N1 8XE

Intermediate Technology Development Group

103–105 Southampton Row
London WCIB 4HH

The Living Earth

86 Colston Street
Bristol BSI 5BB

The National Trust

PO Box 12
Westbury
Wiltshire BA13 4NA

Oxfam

274 Banbury Road
Oxford OX2 7DZ

Royal Society for Nature Conservation

The Green
Nettleham
Lincoln LN2 2NR

Royal Society for the Protection of Birds

The Lodge
Sandy
Bedfordshire SG19 2DL

Survival International

310 Edgware Road
London W2 1DY

Traidcraft

Kingsway
Team Valley Trading Estate
Gateshead
Tyne & Wear
NE11 0NE

World Wide Fund for Nature

Panda House
Weyside Park
Godalming
Surrey GU7 1XR

This book is printed on environment-friendly paper

Text copyright © 1991 Meryl Doney
Line illustrations copyright © 1991 Linda Francis and David Mostyn
Cover illustrations copyright © 1991 David Mostyn

Published by
Lion Publishing plc
Sandy Lane West, Oxford England
ISBN 0 7459 1901 4
Albatross Books Pty Ltd
PO Box 320, Sutherland, NSW 2232, Australia
ISBN 0 7324 0292 X

The photograph on page 22 is from the collection of John and Elizabeth Newson, University of Nottingham. The 'Earth Windows' game on page 24 is taken from Sharing Nature with Children by Joseph Cornell, published by Exley Publications Ltd. The time chart on page 27 is adapted from a Greenpeace leaflet and used with the permission of Greenpeace Ltd.

British Library C.I.P. data applied for

Printed and bound in Thailand